The Resumption of Play

The Resumption of Play

Gary Geddes

QUATTRO BOOKS

The publication of *The Resumption of Play* has been generously supported by the Canada Council for the Arts and the Ontario Arts Council.

 Canada Council   Conseil des arts
for the Arts   du Canada

 ONTARIO ARTS COUNCIL
CONSEIL DES ARTS DE L'ONTARIO
an Ontario government agency
un organisme du gouvernement de l'Ontario

Cover painting: "Ishwar" by Martin Honisch
Cover design: Natasha Shaikh and Diane Mascherin
Typography: Diane Mascherin
Editor: Allan Briesmaster

Library and Archives Canada Cataloguing in Publication

Geddes, Gary, 1940-, author
        The resumption of play / Gary Geddes.

Poems.
ISBN 978-1-927443-87-3 (paperback)

        I. Title.

PS8563.E3R48 2016   C811'.54   C2016-900371-X

Published by Quattro Books Inc.
Toronto
www.quattrobooks.ca

Printed in Canada

Books by Gary Geddes

Poetry:
Poems (1971)
Rivers Inlet (1972)
Snakeroot (1973)
Letter of the Master of Horse (1973)
War & other measures (1976)
The Acid Test (1980)
The Terracotta Army (1984; 2007; 2010)
Changes of State (1986)
Hong Kong (1987)
No Easy Exit (1989)
Light of Burning Towers (1990)
Girl by the Water (1994)
The Perfect Cold Warrior (1995)
Active Trading: Selected Poems 1970–1995 (1996)
Flying Blind (1998)
Skaldance (2004)
Falsework (2007)
Swimming Ginger (2010)
What Does A House Want? (2014)

Fiction:
The Unsettling of the West (1986)

Non-Fiction:
Letters from Managua: Meditations on Politics & Art (1990)
Sailing Home: A Journey through Time, Place & Memory (2001)
*Kingdom of Ten Thousand Things: An Impossible Journey from
    Kabul to Chiapas* (2005)
Drink the Bitter Root: A search for justice and healing in Africa
    (2010; USA, 2011)

Drama:
Les Maudits Anglais (1984)

Translation:

I Didn't Notice the Mountain Growing Dark (1986), poems of Li
   Bai and Du Fu

Criticism:

Conrad's Later Novels (1980)
Out of the Ordinary: Politics, Poetry & Narrative (2009)

Anthologies:

20th-Century Poetry & Poetics (1969, 1973, 1985, 1996, 2006)
15 Canadian Poets Times 3 (1971, 1977, 1988, 2001)
Skookum Wawa: Writings of the Canadian Northwest (1975)
Divided We Stand (1977)
The Inner Ear (1983)
Chinada: Memoirs of the Gang of Seven (1983)
Vancouver: Soul of a City (1986)
Compañeros: Writings about Latin America (1990)
The Art of Short Fiction: An International Anthology (1992; brief
   edition, 2000)
70 Canadian Poets (2014)

Contents

Inshallah

—for the survivors,
for Richard Thomas and all those who suffered or died
at Kuper Island Residential School
and at every other 'Alcatraz'
in Canada

The Resumption of Play

We have art in order not to die of the truth.
—Friedrich Nietzsche

The Resumption of Play

I was digging clams and oysters at low-
tide when they came gathering, uniforms
spotless. I didn't hear the vehicle

arrive, but the crunch of boots on shells
could be distinguished over the sea-wash
and clunk of clams hitting the metal

pail. They dragged me, kicking, one on each arm,
the galvanized vessel left at water's
edge. Grandfather had explained in detail

how clams propel themselves deeper in sand
when threatened. And so I offered thanks
and stood a foot from the hole I'd started

to dig. Against my protests and without
warning or ceremony—father absent
on the hunt, the two elders stricken,

mother wailing and beside herself
—they dropped me like an extricated clam
into the metal bed of the pickup.

I had no idea where we were going,
so few vehicles on the logging road
that smashed its way to our isolated

village. I stopped crying after an hour,
a layer of dust invading nostrils, eyes.
Wind whistled in the trees, my long hair

swirled about wild as Medusa's snakes.
If looks could kill, the driver would regret
his disdainful glances in the rear-view

mirror. I sat on the inflated spare
to soften the jolts, let my anger abate,
and concentrated on the galvanized

pail adrift on the rising tide, a gull
sweeping low to inspect the contents. Stable
from the weight of clams in the bottom

yet vulnerable to wind and current,
the bucket, in minutes, would clear the point,
be struck by a rogue wave, then submerge.

No time to decompress or see the sights,
straight to the harbour where a small boat
waited, engine running. I bit the hand

that tried to lift me from the box. Jesus
H. Christ, teach this piece of shit a lesson
for me. Dragged down the ramp by my hair,

kicking. I like his spirit, said the man
at the helm, exhaling. We'll scrub the dirt
off first, make sure the little bugger's not

white underneath. I knew a couple of English
curses, but the crewman spoke my language,
the last time I'd hear it uttered freely

without fear of consequence. He untied
the lines and let the bow swing out. Don't mind
those guys, he whispered with a wink, they're

under government orders. A light chop
struck the bow. Relax, kid, this trip's a breeze
compared to what awaits you over there.

No point dredging up all this slime,
she says. You're comfortable enough,
why make waves? My partner knows

the answer: the shame, the struggle
with addiction. An Apple Indian complicit
in my own assimilation. Smuggled

into the sheltered professional world,
I ought to let it go. Yet the urge
to rub it in their faces is irresistible,

the Happy Gang, the nice ones buttressed
by their myth of innocence. I'm living proof
the experiment succeeded, guinea pigs

galore. Homer's blind extravagance
attracted me, the fact his madcap tales
were oral: celestial wars, kinky sex

and a free-wheeling tribe of trickster gods
whose antics make the written versions burn:
loss, recurring dreams and retribution.

A concrete path extended from the dock
to the residential school, not a tree
or shrub to soften first impressions

or ease the shock of entry. A trio
of black-clad figures observed my arrival
but said nothing. Not a smile betrayed

their obvious disapproval. Quick nod,
and the female, face framed by a white coif
and black hood, used a stiff rawhide prod

to herd me upstairs to the cold showers.
I stood naked before God, clumps of my hair
strewn on the rough floorboards, soap applied

to my mouth with each protest. As my clothes
retired to the furnace, I was decked out
in the identical duds of the kids

I'd seen in passing, all seated in rows.
A cousin, forefinger pressed to closed lips,
nodded once, no smile, then dropped his gaze.

The server flung some maggoty porridge
on my tray. Half the tiny portion stuck
to the serving spoon, but was dislodged

by a forefinger, the same one she'd used
to pick her nose. At least she smiled at me,
my head no higher than her apron pocket.

Not so, the laundry staff, distributing
the ration of clean clothes each week. Seventh
in line, I'd forgotten my number when

I was jabbed in the back and three English
syllables whispered in my ear. Snickers
from the older boys as I repeated the sounds:

six-tee-nine. The laughter cost James,
my cousin, three days lock-up in the cellar
on bread and water. Gaunt when released,

he managed a triumphant grin which earned
him two more days of jail-time in the dark.
I practiced memorizing in my sleep.

I tried to make myself invisible,
mouthing, ad nauseam, foreign words
the teachers repeated, pedagogy

not their strongest suit. Flash cards containing
pertinent nouns and verbs had not occurred
to them. Illustrations neither. Older kids

had to repeat the English word or phrase
on the board, mime each object and action.
The boy from Ahousaht barked twice, lifted

his leg and mimed a dog urinating
on the teacher's desk. This touching antic
(a lesson we'd not forget) cost the clever

thespian his lunch and three hours chopping
wood. No thought of syntax, sentence structure,
just words tossed out like worthless trade beads. Still

I ingested this new language, mostly
in secret, a glutton for syllables,
knowing them the key to my survival.

According to books, human behaviour
repeats itself. Not exactly good news
for a captive audience of children.

In Dickens' *Great Expectations*, a kid,
his life overturned, is dangled upside down
in the graveyard by an escaped convict.

I learned fast to question the distinctions
between criminal and cop, predator
and priest. Another native Pip-squeak

launched on a cockeyed journey, a high
learning curve where survival depends
on the ability to dance and adapt,

make split-second decisions, bridle
emotions. Once in captivity,
you cultivate the miscreant within,

teach yourself to interpret dreams, be
useful, so those in charge will hesitate
to harm, or chuck you in the lions' den.

Mine was the first hand raised in question
period, the teacher wanting to know
the number of feet and yards in a mile.

Dead easy. 1760 yards, I said. And feet?
5280 feet in a mile, unless there are a dozen
Indian kids walking that mile, which brings

the total number of feet to 5304, or less
if one is missing a limb. Father's Irish
face registered surprise, then outrage,

ordering me to the front of the class
where he placed my hands on the desk, pulled
down my pants and underwear, and applied

the strap a dozen times, sermonizing
on the evils of being a smart aleck.
Whether the humiliation was worse

than the pain I don't recall, but the small
river of urine, whose headwaters gathered
at my unwashed feet, earned another five.

It took three weeks for the ruptured skin
to heal. I was sent to the sick room, forced
to bunk-in with a tubercular kid,

a death sentence, a one-way ticket
to the Indian hospital. The angry ulcers
on his neck and chest were gift-wrapped

in rough cotton, but oozing yellow pus
stank and left its mark on the pillowcase
we shared. Afraid to speak, Tom wrote

his name on a tiny scrap of paper.
Prayers to the Creator and another,
for good measure, to the Lucky Jesus

seemed to work. Infection did not set in.
My bed-mate, alas, not so fortunate,
died, age ten, in the nearby hospital.

I was back in my dorm lying doggo.
Tom's death went unrecorded at the school
and rumours said he never rose again.

Kill the Indian in the child, Scott's
"final solution." Remove both parents,
culture, language, replace them with perverts,

sociopaths. Incompetents in lieu
of elders, sad stories of tortured saints
and crucifixions sterile substitutes

for Raven with his corrugated cardboard
laugh. We had common myths of origin,
though ours breathed humour, employed a cast

of rascals more like the Greek pantheon.
We shared, also, the turning of humans
into stone, though Native legends make this

a tribute to enduring love or reward
for good stewardship, not a penalty
for folly, disobedience. Values

from home instilled by living example,
not fear of punishment, are what I recall,
squatting in the ember's luminous glow.

Since overachieving did not sit well
with fellow inmates, I squandered my time
in daydreams, imagining the straightest

pole, carving the broader end to receive
a bone or metal tip, gut-tied. Spearing
salmon in the stream at spawning season

proved a highlight for my father, brothers
and me, equidistant along the banks,
competing with black bear and eagle

for the sea's bounty. Flash of silver scales,
a fierce passion to reproduce turning
the underbelly blood-red, the sleek jaw

to a snarl. An unschooled cub, current
and dexterous fish thwarting his desire,
monitored my movements from the other

bank. I flipped him a sockeye, which he caught
in mid-air and, teeth bared, carted off
amongst cedars and moss-covered nurse logs.

At night the cold and foul air in the dorm
kept us awake. Frozen drains, toilets backed
up, resulted in a brigade of buckets

brimming with piss and excrement.
Plungers did not work and the maintenance
staff had other priorities. Effluent

was carted down several flights of stairs
and dumped in the garden plot. Cabbage
was gigantic that summer, but we refused

to eat it, night soil a foreign notion
at the time. The youngsters, in whose numbers
I include myself, who managed to spill

this mouth-watering concoction, spent
the whole day on hands and knees scrubbing stairs
and floor with disinfectant so watered

down it helped distribute germs in the grains
of unpainted wood. A crowning moment
to cherish later, blest alma mater.

Government, unimpressed, cut rations,
costs. Too little food, substandard teachers.
The new regime would be more rigorous,

half the day in class, half in the garden
tending produce for the market, chickens
busting a gut to deliver eggs, large

brown ones we could only eat by stealth,
blaming the shortages on otters, rats,
neurotic hens. Every whiff of fresh air

kindled thoughts of home and inspired
escapes. Logs lashed together with scarves
carried two girls as far as the white shell

midden, their swamped brown bodies intertwined,
such unforeseen affection found in death.
School on high alert after that, sermons

on misbehaviour and God's will, garden
duty supervised, beatings commonplace,
a harvest of bruises and wet beds.

It's not what I intended, this litany
of abuse. The realization came
during a Composition class. I'd spent

the hour teaching kids the correct
use of pronouns: Don't say "her and me are
going," but "she and I." When I told them

"her" and "me" are used as objects of verbs
and prepositions, as in "they killed her"
or "sock it to me," all eyes glazed over

and one of them whispered a word I'd never
heard before: *kurrintenshizen*. Explain
for the edification of the class,

I demanded. Please, sir—Gertrude, blonde hair,
Marlene Dietrich pose—it's German, sir,
I'll write it down and leave it on your desk.

Buzzer, ebbing tide of laughter, tightly
folded scrap of paper. The translation:
too tight-assed to shit a currant. Bingo!

It wasn't always so, my sphincter stretched
and penetrated. Schoolyard fun and games
suspended, waiting for the holy Father

to shout a number from his open window.
God has much for you to learn, he said,
applying the Vaseline. No mention

what the lesson was, though I surmised
it had to do with power, authority.
As he drove his point home, I could hear

the resumption of play, a low murmur
rising slowly like an organ bass outside.
He insisted I recite the Lord's Prayer

as he went about his business. My turns
were infrequent as he had other
favourites. Time for the shame to burn off

and bury myself in the books of Greek
mythology he loaned me from his shelf.
And so my education was advanced.

A clam, the textbook explains, has a mouth,
kidney, anus, but no heart. No wonder
I felt such affinity for this bivalve

mollusc that uses abductor muscles
to yank its half shells tight at the slightest
threat. Like them, I clam up in social

situations, keep my mouth shut even
as the puns accumulate, emotions
run rampant. I prefer the privacy

of high tide, avoid the phallic geo-
duck clam so rich in amino acids
and testosterone-producing zinc.

The horny marine biologist next door
scares the living daylight out of me.
A sick heart's the obvious exception

as it can endure a decade or more
in lock-up, another running full speed,
and still supply the vital organs blood.

Escaping the Church was never easy,
even in the workplace. School breaks
I spent at the refinery loading

boxcars with 100-pound sacks of sugar
and riding a vertical conveyor belt,
No protection, only a series of steps

and handles. Inelegant, unrefined,
it was at least uplifting and whisked
us floor to floor. Called a paternoster lift

because its junctions mimicked special beads
in the rosary, spaced at intervals
as reminders to repeat the Our Father,

this crude but elevating contraption proved
an unexpected blessing, warning us
of the foreman's imminent arrival.

We paid homage to the speed of sound,
1200 feet per second, which caused the hymns
he hummed to reach us long before he did.

We called the school Alcatraz, but life
in a maximum security pen
would have been easier: no forced labour,

the food better and more abundant,
and the possibility of parole. When
my friend Richard reached the leaving age,

he blew his chances with an overheard
phone call to his sister, in which he vowed
to spill the beans to the authorities.

He was found the next morning in the gym
hanging by his neck from a rafter, tongue
swollen and extended. The priest marched us

past with the warning that this is what big
mouths can expect. We discovered later,
schools closed and the files at last opened,

Richard's murder was described as suicide
to the cops, but the coroner's report
listed the cause of death as strangulation.

In a dream Grandmother is bent over
picking camas root, sea blush, mimulus,
a.k.a. monkey flower, for herbal

remedies. We're on the rocky islet
we used to laugh and call Eden. No snakes,
either friendly or mythical, soil enough

for a few junipers, a struggling oak,
stone crop, a plethora of native plants.
We're being entertained by oyster-

catchers with their orange bills and hip-hop
sound and an amorous pair of brown-headed
cowbirds. They mate for life, Grandma said,

females as usual doing all the work,
but they're not good parents, notorious
for laying their eggs in other's nests. Brood

parasites, they're also known as obligates:
lacking the memory of how to build
a nest. Or was the word recalled Oblates?

For years I took refuge in alcohol,
the occult, and Rudolf Steiner's writings,
which enabled me to project myself

beyond the physical realm, to think
this earthly state a mortal training ground
for the hereafter, blaming all illness

on the dark forces of the double, the
Mephistophelian presence that invades
the infant's body at birth and exerts

its foul control. Physical love, he advised,
diminishes us, causes us to stray,
stop short of the divine, which, oddly,

he found rooted in Russian soil, whence
the Great Light emanated. America,
he warned, had been blocked off for centuries

to safeguard us from the deadly seeds
of savagery, materialism, greed.
Us and *them*, the treachery of pronouns.

Steiner's essay "Geographic Medicine"
healed nothing. In fact, it blamed the victims,
not the perpetrators preaching mumbo-jumbo

to a would-be intelligentsia
who abandoned reason for theosophy.
Electric streams, Ahrimanic forces,

then the blatant assertion that Europe
needed protection from the "differently
constituted" race of Indians, products

obviously of earthly magnetism,
whatever. This brief, insane quotation
liberated me, naming old hatreds,

explaining the treachery, betrayal
of stewardship. And to think it written
in 1917, less than two decades

before the European Jews learned
how it feels to be an Indian, an object
of interest, chosen for extermination.

Belittled and browbeaten, rage turned
inward: drink, abuse, the beloved's face
damaged beyond repair. Poundmaker

and Big Bear had starvation and Gatling
guns to temper their resistance, treaties
the only option. My broken cellmates

weren't exactly masters of their fate, nor
captains of their soul. Buffaloed, driven
over the edge, extinction was their name.

Or Charley Joe, dishevelled, diabetic,
hooked on all the adjectives he couldn't
afford, asleep, his head on my shoulder,

a soft erratic snore. When I was tossed
into the drunk tank, Charley offered me
his ragged sweater and told me about

his little sister, working the streets
in Kelowna, missing, but born with dimples
from the Creator's thumb and forefinger.

I tried Maoist politics, another drug
that left me empty. If power corrupts,
it also disrupts the work of healing.

The Brits provided opium, then screwed
the Chinese royally. Bullets and booze
were good enough for us, along with Jesus,

beads and smallpox blankets. Stench of rot
drifted for miles, the sky black with turkey
vultures. Not a pretty site, but ripe for sharks,

speculators. An archival photograph
shows the pustuled face of my great-great
grandfather, sepia tones softening the pain

and outrage in his eyes. This selfsame game,
still played, goes by the name of real estate,
real, one of the scariest English words.

We're taught to love our neighbours as ourselves,
but how to accomplish this exalted task
when told that you're a worthless piece of shit.

A Ph.D. cured me of the desire
for academia. Piled High and Deep.
Some joke. Besides, I'd already had

the third degree. I needed another sort
of doctoring, the kind that heals, not hours
spent in the library ghosting the stacks

for reference books, trying to forget.
Rules bent to accommodate Indians
in the system: First Nations, the first

shall be last, a minority, not-quite-
visible. Union card in hand, I snagged
a job in Sudbury, an inferno of slag

resurfaced to approximate parkland,
the same kind of cosmetic procedure
I'd used in my flight from Alcatraz.

Turtlenecks instead of suits or cassocks,
a tribute to the continent called home,
and my own small tribe of non-believers.

I remember a conference in D.C.
where Milton scholars worldwide gathered,
resolved to celebrate the genius

of this old, blind poet, not exactly
a saint according to wife and children,
but driven to justify the ways of God

to men, first of all to himself. Panel
I-8, the hotel's smallest seminar
room, where I met the moderator

and other panellists, the room not exactly
packed. The audience consisted of two
African women in colourful robes

and three men, one of whom, realizing
his mistake, left in search of a session
on Milton's politics. I sympathized,

loving the poet's republicanism.
I shared his scorn for Royals, monarchy,
but not his anti-Irish bigotry.

You think the healing complete, old wounds
licked clean. When my son's unthinking comment
evoked a sharp rebuke, I felt myself

grow small in the reversed binoculars
of his eyes, affection losing ground to fear.
Gravel churned in the driveway, then the peel

of tires on asphalt, the last sound I'd hear
before the sirens and the flashing lights.
Where to put my face? The old familiar

shame. That "stupid Indian" again. Detox
saved me, for a few weeks, from looking her
in the eye. My shrink was sympathetic

but never seemed to understand the source.
He thought religion, or a holiday,
might do the trick. I picnicked in hell,

found refuge in my garden, tests to grade,
and planned to spend the summer reading books
like Armstrong's *Slash* and Dee Brown's *Wounded Knee.*

And there they were, a gallery of chiefs
tucked away in a dirty-brown paperback:
Little Crow, Tatanka (Sitting Bull),

and Big Foot photographed in death, face
incredulous, even his outstretched arms
frozen in disbelief. I re-read their speeches,

outraged as each was betrayed and died
violently, promises broken, treaties
written in bad faith, the slow genocide

clearly deliberate. A few good friends,
John Clum, agent, and Edward Wynkoop,
Major, who confessed he'd felt himself

in the presence of superior beings.
I studied my face, framed by liquor bottles
in the bar mirror, to see if I could catch

a glimpse of something superior, took
a leave of absence from my teaching job,
blew kisses to the brats I'd come to love.

What to do with anger and with shame?
I was blinder than Homer, with stories
no one wanted to hear, a ragged script

wrestling its way to clarity. Blindness
has its virtues, I suppose. It forces you
to listen, to feel the air electric,

the body's light that makes the hair rise
and move like eelgrass in a tidal pool.
Eyes widened at the pub to hear me speak

of moral turpitude, sexual abuse,
murder in God's name, and the churches
failed instruments of the divine. Enough

sermons, my buddies jeered. More beer,
less bullshit. I drunkenly complied.
Sound advice from hell's beleaguered saints,

disciples all, whose uncloistered virtues
surpass, so liberally scattered, their teacher's
morbid litanies. Sadder, Budweiser.

Chances of survival were fifty-fifty
in the residential school. Unmarked graves
contained the bones of infants, aborted

by the nuns, and children dead from beatings
or disease, immune systems compromised
by hunger, loneliness. A decade spent

viewing the world through a haze of drugs
and alcohol, my children neglected,
my wife driven to distraction. When AA

meetings failed, I yielded to the sweat lodge,
feeling the anger seep out through my pores,
the stone begin to lift from my chest.

Good news for Sisyphus. A year to dry out,
with the help of friends, song, drumming, dance,
all of us scarred, bearing the marks of war.

Nursed, embraced, encouraged to go back,
take the children with me. I didn't know
if I could do it, or if I wanted to.

I returned home a stranger. The paved road
held no magic, the trees no longer spoke
to me. Father lost at sea. Mother, overcome

by grief and joy, did not know how to say
it in my new language. Grandfather smiled
and placed a metal bucket by my chair.

When I did not respond, he picked it up
and dragged his crippled body to the shore
to dig for clams. The tide was out. The sea,

a looking-glass, reflected our mutual
despair. I walked to water's edge,
touched his shoulder and gently eased

the shovel from his hands. As I applied
my weight to the blade and felt it cut deep,
the tidal funk awoke some feelings long

submerged and I found myself weeping
and laughing at the same time, a creature
naked, shucked, fit for neither sea nor land.

Speak to the Wound

Alas I did not say what I should have . . .
And form itself as always is betrayal.
　　　　　—Czesław Miłosz

Late Breaking News

We're in Wally's Renault, driving
south in Provence, the car radio
harvesting disaster, swaths of it,

and the fields bloody with tulips,
a brash statement stretching
to the low hills of the Luberon.

Later, in the hilltop fortress
with its catapult and trebuchet,
I ask my friend what happened

to monks, to sanctuary, places
where little pain sears the weary
breastbone, where envy's rare

as gourmet meals, where even
the spirited horse, grown
accustomed to lassitude, nudges

the pitchfork's worn handle until
hay falls like manna from the loft,
and where prayers are crafted

in lieu of weapons. Eternity
is long, Pascal has written, so
faith is worth the gamble.

The soul sets sail for a distant
port. Tears mark its departure,
but what marks its arrival?

Planks resound with footsteps,
deep water parts to accommodate
the insistent keel. Wally, amused,

dismisses these speculations,
insists there's romance
in neither monastery nor rose.

Solace, perhaps, though skimpy,
and only in what the moving pen
inscribes or the stiff horsehairs

of the brush render permanent
and lovely, those moments, all
too brief, when the anchor holds

and the sea blooms resplendent
with species of kelp and with the
scrubbed tulip faces of the dead.

Virginia, Streaming

I feared the transformation mental illness
brings, how it takes you to the precipice,

the void, yet commands so little space
in literature. As heavy as the abstractions

it gathers in its wake, a sick mind
packs a hellish punch, empties the guilt-

banker's account, knocks the stuffing out
of accountant and scarecrow alike.

For days at a time my talking did not stop,
drifting in and out of coherence. Words

and sentences, so chiselled and succinct
in my prose, collapsed in a heap, a jumble

not even Leonard could decipher. Periodic
mood swings led to *tete-à-tetes* with birds

in Greek, the mind a room of its own
with dreadful clutter and the blitz of unwelcome

guests. Open windows and barbiturates
beckoned, barbarians at the gate, Battle

of Britain nerves, cranial explosions, insomnia,
memory of intimate invasions even by those

I trusted, brotherly love a mockery.
Illness, for me, defied metaphor, so real,

so palpable, compounded by stress, loss—
a sister, a mother, our wartime houses

bombed. And dear Septimus, back from France,
arms and legs intact, a casualty nonetheless,

shell-shocked, unhinged, temple in ruins.
Me again, prescient, writing my death

in a soldier's suicide, a liberating act
for those left behind, Leonard, Mrs. D.

A pocketful of stones, coat and hat placed
neatly by the water's edge. In my ears

the blood pounds arterial, artillery, a front
to be defended, Ouse, the stream

of consciousness, breaking the surface,
the syntax, don't go, don't go, the whole cast

standing to wave, Roger, Julia, Mother, O-
phelia, full fathom five, a cupful all you need.

Brown Out

That moment when the lights dim,
and appliances—sturdy, reliable—shudder
as if to some private ecstasy, resume
their steady, comforting electrical hum,

cloaking the silence, old feelings
of tenderness and hurt tucked neatly
into zip-lock bags. Crystallized fibres
exuding freezer-breath. A sperm-

bank of the emotions. Green peppers
by the sackful, free-range chickens.
This ain't *Gunsmoke*, Pardner!
Ahm gonna run those persnickety

Bard Rocks and Rhode Island Reds
outa town. Pain threshold.
Up in smoke. Where the buffalo.
Rome wasn't. Damn it,

I tried. Programmed responses,
a surge suppressor, dark glasses.
Biting down on a sucking-stone
whenever he wants it. Freeze,

suppress, re-program, no Girl Guide
better prepared. Betrayed
by some digital clock in my eyes
flashing 12:00. All that training,

regimentation, matrimonial boot camp,
5BX, indoctrination via movies,
video. And still the shit comes
down. No blue-black body art, face

rearranged like a Picasso. We're
not talking physical violence
here. The eyes tell more than time.
Other ways to skin a cat.

Dangling Participle

All afternoon spent teaching the little snits
participles. Rhymes with nipples.
Yesterday was gerunds. Care less? I doubt

they remember the basic definitions.
Hormones? Scratched on the blackboard:
"The John enters, the whore moans"

Another day: "SIN TAX." Progress,
the department head grinned,
wanting me, his wife and three kids

waiting in the station wagon. *Headway*,
giving head. Even with her British accent,
the new Anglican minister offends me

with her incorrect usage: *enervate*,
when obviously she means energize,
and "should have went." Queen's

English, right. She should have went
to Grammar School, not seminary. Moral?
Never underestimate the colonies.

3:00 a.m. Gridwork shadows. Drugstore
neon filters through my rattled
blinds. Sounds of aluminium rigging

when he took me at the yacht club.
Frigging, et cetera. Shorthand, vowels
not the only things swallowed

in the heart's vernacular. I woke
from a tryst, speaking in tongues, pure
gibberish, ecstatic, soaked,

unfinished, thinking: Why
should I feel guilty, this is *my* dream,
I'll fuck whomever I want.

Speak to the Wound

B is comforting a friend
after work, coffee gone cold,
ashtray brimming, the cigarette
in her right hand scribing a bold arc
in the dark of December.

So, tell me about it,
she says. No judgment here,
just a sympathetic ear
for as long as you need it.
All those embarrassing actions
and thoughts. I've got enough to go around
for both of us. Did I ever tell you
about last summer? Yah, well, you know me,
sainthood was not my career goal.

I wanted to crap out, leave my husband,
kids, job. No shit, just bugger off
and see what freedom tasted
like. I got as far as Safeway.
Symbolic, eh? The bold, red letters
on the supermarket froze me in my tracks.

Speak to the wound, the phrase
Lao Tzu used, knowing the injuries inside
that fester unhealed,
not just the bruised ego, slighted
by rejection, but the hurt
that is bottomless, beyond
memory. The friend shaking, hugging
herself for warmth, rocking,

and B, already diagnosed
with cancer of the throat, fingers
of one hand spread on the chequered oilcloth,
listens in the cigarette's glow.

Assignment

Sunlight reflected off her ebony face, slightly
oiled, narrow brow, shaved head
bent to the task.

She could go back, recall the details,
seven men in military uniforms
fumbling with their trousers, standing
in line as if waiting to be paid.

No periods, the surgery
redone three times, headaches
a constant.

Not one of them looked me in the eye,
she said.

I adjusted my ass
on the chair, fumbled
another question.

My husband? An unpaid teacher
working in the mines.

She scooped a small stick
from the ground, rolled it several times
between her fingers, then
snapped it in half.

Nuggets of wisdom, he used
to say. When the soldiers
finished with me, my feet and legs
were swimming in his blood.

I turned the tape recorder off,
replaced my notebook in the knapsack,
camera an albatross on my back.
What to do with my face
was the problem.

A motorcycle revved
outside the compound, coughed,
the needle valve set a turn
too rich.

What to say as a member
of this other species, pathetic,
retrograde? I forced myself
to look her in the eye.

Blues for Kony

I told the *muzungu* my story, a reporter
I presumed. He wanted all the details
I could remember. Okay, I said. Yes,
there was pain, but that's not the worst

part. Besides these holes in my face
there is a vast hole in the universe
called the future, with no place
for the mutilated. Without my ears

I can still hear. Cutting off my nose
did not affect my sense of smell. Lips,
I discovered soon enough, are not made
to kiss, but to hold food in the mouth

while it's being chewed. A hand clasped
over my face serves two purposes:
enables me to eat and covers the shame.
Unlike the sister seated on my left,

I was not forced to kill my husband
in front of the children or serve as whore-
de-camp. Pregnant, I survived, God
knows why. Perhaps they had orders,

a logic that escaped me. The severed
parts, a bloody pulp thrust in my hands,
disgusted me, but I couldn't bear to toss
them in the bush. *Human rights,* that

was the phrase the reporter used
before slipping the ballpoint pen in a vest
pocket and closing his blue ring-binder
like a schoolboy anticipating recess.

As he unravelled his legs from the chair
and rose to leave, he asked a final
question, still unable to look at me:
What's needed to stop this carnage,

bring Kony's monsters to the courts?
Ah, justice. A quaint abstraction. Abducted
boys in posh jail cells in The Hague,
clutching a remote control instead of

an AK-47, watching vehicles blow up
in Kinshasa, Kandahar, London, Abidjan?
Bring them home, let the healing begin,
discharge a tender reconciliation.

Intertidal

Art is our chief means of breaking bread with the dead.
— W. H. Auden

At Swim Three Words

As mother lay dying in a dark, cold
room, plumbing and ductwork were visible
overhead, and cracks in cement walls sprouted
spiderwebs and dust. I recall the flume

at the Ex that flung us headlong, risible
in the extreme, plunging down the chute
like hell's hounds into the shrieking crowd.
Mouth wide, kerchief blown back, her body

language quizzical as if laughter were
verboten, out of bounds, a joker outed
sans warning. When I stood by the bed,
my small hand clasped in hers, I had grounds

to wonder if she would die, though I doubted
this, of course, thinking only of myself,
my needs, days at the beach in English Bay
or Kits, where I tossed sand, flouted

authority, sun-baked bodies, the air
reeking of seaweed, chips, vinegar, hot
dogs. Some days I feel her speak through me,
the few remaining strands of damp, brown hair

at sixes and sevens across her forehead,
lips pursed, facial muscles contracted
in a worry. Mortal counsel, endnotes,
obligatory whispers with their dread

finality. Resolute, I played the elf,
doing the dog-paddle across the frayed
linoleum, trying to make her laugh.
A tad of whimsy left on the back shelf

would suffice. She rallied briefly, half
alert, pulled herself into a sitting
position, skin slack around her neck, eyes
closed from the effort. Grimace or laugh,

I knew not, but she who swam kilometres
from Fisherman's Cove to Point Atkinson
managed a thin smile, patted my head and
traced on my back the necessary letters.

The Celebrity

Mother dressed to the nines, high
heels, beige wool suit, hair piled up
at back. Fit to kill. And so they did,

the doctors, the cells, the primitive
equipment. Cancer ward, VGH, post-
war medics, a health squad of warriors

armed with radium tubes, hit-and-miss
fluoroscopes. If uranium can take out
two Japanese cities and end a long war,

it can surely handle, properly directed,
a few wayward cells. We'd call this
target practice, except you don't get

a second chance. Radiation therapy
intended to shrink the uterine tumour.
What to expect when these gadgets

were still being used in stores, kids
shocked and delighted to see the skeletal
outline of their bones inside a new pair

of shoes. In the waiting room, I thumb
the pages of *Life, Saturday Evening Post*,
thinking how important my mother

must be, getting all this attention, nurses
dropping by to chat and cheer me up,
my short legs two frenetic pendula

pumping beneath the square chrome
tubing of the chair, the promise
of ice cream post-op. Mother

there amongst the great names,
Roentgen, Becquerel, Curie, but no call
from the Nobel Committee for her,

only an early death at 35, and no record
of where her radioactive ashes went
at Mount Pleasant Crematorium,

but, still, she had the style and sense
of occasion to expire on Valentine's
Day, a mini-triumph, a heart-stopper.

Matricide

You were the death of her,
Gran confides, pouring hot water
into a quarter cup of milk.
Cambric tea, she calls it.

Words, the one thing Gran
does not mince. Good English
straight-talk, mollycoddle and
bamboozle not found in her

vocabulary. This info offered me
as a boy of eleven, absent four years
in the prairies after your demise.
Dr. Dykes, it seems, warned you

not to get pregnant; you didn't
listen, that wayward star
still in the East. A lump of honey,
spoon clasped in a gnarled

arthritic claw, the cacophony
of stirring. I weigh the import
of what she tells me, where
to store it, and how to conduct

my new life as a criminal,
which makes my lies and self-abuse
pale by comparison. The delicate
china cup with gold-rimmed

lip and scalloped circumference
shakes in my hand and rattles
as it docks with the saucer.
Mugs from here on, or mug shots,

second degree, parole proscribed,
transportation, convict ship
to Australia or Mars, intergalactic
penal colony. It all makes sense

now, especially the word *penal*
from which these problems,
both yours and mine, appear
to derive. How language betrays

you, a slip of the tongue
or a tongue in the ear. I place
my fingers on the bible she keeps
beside the teapot, raise my hand

and swear. Yes, I swear I'll bear
this stigma like a stoic, devote
myself to keeping your memory
alive by making poems. So, help me.

Traceries

The names you carried:
Hazel Lillian Irene, their nod
to origins, where it all
began. Seed, ovum,

countless millennia, a slew
of spermutations bringing us
together. The Phoenix, ashen,
rises again from its pyre

transformed, protean.
I inherit the genetic code,
weak chin, strong opinions,
the river running through

your veins, its untold
narratives. You weren't Helen
though your smile launched
a thousand packages

from the display wagon
at Eaton's: Miss Wrigley's
Spearmint Gum. Something
for an offspring to chew

on. Where did it all go,
the two bulldogs, faces so ugly
only a mother or small child
could love absolutely.

Making room, as if the space
were somehow finite?
Thanks for the inscription,
DNA and all, passing it on,

not a page blank, but volumes
with notes in the margins,
whole libraries, and a key
to the stacks in Alexandria.

Salvage

I drive past the old home
in Kerrisdale, its promptings unclear,
to capture perhaps a clue, some
fragment of the past, 44th

and Maple, trees long gone,
third house from the corner,
a wide veranda, inside
the living room an enclosed

glass cabinet where the ceramic
cookie jar was kept, fluted
white enamel, rose pattern
and gold edges. I recall no light

or joy in that house. Vague
recollections of a gathering,
pipe smoke, small talk, crepe
streamers. How did it feel,

illness drawing you back
in full retreat to the home-place?
So many questions. Photos
of happier days, you and Pat,

young girls in pale blouses
and scalloped skirts on the lawn,
peas in a pod, stockings
to match, hair in ringlets,

embracing two bulldogs.
Today I'd notice the slippage,
distillation, body and spirit
moving to essence,

the old sawdust burner
pumping its heart out. Never
enough heat, enough time.
I could knock, introduce

myself, an old man nostalgic
for the mother he scarcely
knew. You grew up here, familiar
with its crooks and nannies,

special hiding places, a poetics
of space, stairs to the unfinished
attic, rafters bare, no insulation,
the forbidden trunk, its lost

cargo of correspondence.
Dog days. Not hot, just Sirius,
Scotty struck on the Boulevard,
his body lowered among the gnarled

roots of the quince. And Wallace
Stevens, losses notwithstanding, dreams
of Susanna, of Peter Quince at the clavier,
fingers spidering the keyboard.

Bent over, how to lace shoes,
laughing as your fine, brown hair
brushes my face. I envy those
ugly bulldogs their embrace.

September Song

Months in the care of friends as white cells
multiplied and grains of fine sand dwindled
in the upper chamber of the hourglass.

Too sensitive, they concluded, to attend
your funeral—well-meaning, but wrong.
Afterwards, on the landing, your fingers

wringing the striped apron. No telltale signs,
only a shy, apologetic smile. Not quite
enough. Instead, I swam in urine

for a year, my eyes rolled and the nights, yes,
they grew long, bedsheets refusing to dry
in cold air. A boat passes, reflected

light flickers on the ceiling like tag-ends
of a projected film in black & white.
Saccharin lyrics, choked with pathos

but the chorus haunts, a melody you played
on the piano while I swam submerged
in placental waters, playing my own

waiting game. You gaze at me from the face
of my youngest daughter, the one who seems
to hear a different story, a subtext

or parallel narrative, when I speak to her.
And so, this persistent chinwag, words
a substitute umbilicus, each letter

an increment of desire, a subterfuge
to keep us conjoined, in cahoots, co-
conspirators, serving this life sentence.

Breakage

If I could find the canister
they kept your ashes in

I'd re-assemble dust
and bone as once I tried

to reconstruct that heap
of photos chopped

in pieces by my former
tenants. They'd vacated

the dwelling as abruptly
as their marriage ended,

he taking up with a fellow-
worker at the casino;

she, amidst tears and curses,
destroying every image

of their lives together.
Alone again, I couldn't

bear the dissolution
and sat at the glass-top

table beneath the skylight,
their domestic jigsaw

spread out in front,
my eyes brimming,

photos with daddy
removed, an arm

or disembodied hand,
hanging on for not-so-dear

life, head obliterated
by a burning cigarette

or compass point.
Your own departure, less

abrupt, still brought down
the house, the mort

in mortgage. The slots
have names: Goldfish, Texas Tea

and Hangover. But that One-
armed Bandit won't bring you

back, nor the canister
of charred remains, my

erstwhile host and
residence.

Intertidal

Evenings when the tide is low and my paddle
scrapes rocks or drags in mud, when gulls
head home, last shell of the day clamped tight
in their beaks, when purple stars loosen
their grip on submerged logs or barnacles

and prepare to swim again in the night sky,
I think of you, made-up, hair in a bun, at work
as a demonstrator, smiling, your heart going out
for chewing gum, mayonnaise or latest brand
of crackers, two kids at home, latch-key

specials emptying the last lick from the jar
of peanut butter. Already some terminal
signs, spotting, the pain and swelling still
to come, how to know, then, it was serious,
each visit to the doctor another day

without pay. As the channel deepens, I bite
into the darkness, catch the muffled voice
of water thrust astern, a rumble so faint
I turn to see who's following me, imagine
shift nurses discussing your condition

in hushed tones, the shaking of heads, all
that knowledge useless now. I balance
my paddle across the cockpit for a moment
and drift till silence overcomes the petty
turbulence, letting the current do the work.

A Song of Recall

And so it is with longing, you extend a hand
into the mist expecting to take hold of something
lost, perhaps the very thing you'd yearned for

but could not claim, a dream-shape, an unwritten
melody, insistent, that flitted in and out of your days
leaving its residue on your pillow, the faint smear

on an otherwise blank page, a colophon of desire.
You glimpse an apron, blue, with a pale, stitched
hem, a smudge of flour near the generous pocket,

enough to hold for a moment that lost mother
disappearing into the night who might, just might
be yours, wisps of her long dark hair surviving

cancer, surviving the flames, making a mockery
of memory itself, that insatiable canvas needing
to be filled, framed, needing to have occurred.

On Being Dead in Venice

It was awesome and liberating
to play a Russian spy.
—Lucas Till

Vodorosli

for Joseph Brodsky

Late morning, little traffic, Venetian crows
soft-pedalling in the ornamental cedars,
Adriatic cul-de-sac. Brodsky at rest,

passport in order, papers in the archive. His grave's
a mess from all the visitors. A mandala dangles
from his headstone by a leather cord.

Beside the slab a flask of vodka half empty
and a little plastic pail of ballpoint pens. A dozen
roses with a business card, signed: Mr. X,

Collector of Fine Art, phone number in New York.
No judges here or KGB to label him a parasite. After
Visconti's *Death in Venice*, Brodsky dreamt of ending it

on a San Marco waterway, using, with all due irony,
a Browning revolver. Instead of dying in Venice,
he did the next best thing, took out permanent residence.

He had his favourites. Pound wasn't one, despite
translations and a shared enthusiasm for "making it new."
They'd never met, only Olga, keeper of the flame,

toeing the party line: no fascism, no anti-Semitism.
Ezra's a Jewish name, she argued. Neighbours now,
not rivals, Joseph the new kid on the block.

Beauty: a stay against forgetting, loss, the illusion
of timelessness. Venice, he said in *Watermark*,
dissolves the self. It's palazzi with their portraits,

putti and porphyry: sunken treasures best viewed
underwater, eyes wide, mouth shut tight.
The latter mode proved difficult: a hectoring teacher,

confrontational, dismissive. All that bluster kept at bay
the self-disgust and insecurities of youth, the tortured
English, a struggle even Stockholm could not cure.

I recall his observation that illness is the end
of metaphor. He'd been writing about Sontag,
their visit to Olga, the Gaudier-Brzeska bust

of Pound nearby, Susan with her cancer, Joseph
fighting (discarded cigarette filters notwithstanding)
heart disease. A touching moment, two naked selves

eroding, swathed in history, both present, both departed.
What goings-on these ballpoint pens would tell us
if they could. I bring the smell of *vodorosli*,

a clump of seaweed, rank, scraped from Rialto's
steps. Mortality, the tidal musk of sex.
We write in water, mark our passing with an X.

Not To Be Upstaged

Rimsky-Korsakov dumped my first compositions
in a waste bin in St. Petersburg. Not polite,
but definitely useful. It made me angry,
determined to leave him in my dust. Paris

beckoned. I abandoned Law and my literary
journal to pursue art on the world's stage. Music
would be the handmaiden of theatre, dance,
design. I had a nose for what is new and how

to market it, a tribute to my merchant bloodlines.
The cognoscenti were eating out of my hand
in short order, know-it-alls vying for attention
from Sergei, the rogue prodigal, maestro

of Les Ballets Russes. I was God for an hour.
Debussy wrote the score for *Jeux,* young men
and women cavorting on stage in search of a lost
tennis ball. Balls, more likely. Hardly subtle,

but it kept them moving—actors and the viewer's
eye—with amazing choreography, sets designed
by Picasso, Braque, Matisse. My beloved
Nijinksy, so wonderfully endowed, wowed them

with his suggestive movements, *un succès
de scandale.* And I adored Vaslav, privately
of course, refused to soil a gift in which I found
such pleasure. I, who lost my mother at birth,

nursed his talent, weaned him reluctantly.
Igor called him weak, said he made love
only to the nymph's scarf in *Afternoon of a Faun.*
Rite of Spring caused a riot in 1913, Igor

striking an insolent lout in the foyer. I loved it,
the ballet and the ensuing battle of the critics
who called me evil, modern, criminal, obscene.
I made no apologies for the sex or sacred

calling. Dima, Leo, Boris, Anton, their genius
seduced me. Submission or dominance—what
do they matter if art is the ultimate surrender?
All my lovers married, or left me for other men.

As I expired in Venice on August 19, 1929
I rallied enough to say: "Friends, Sergei is staging
a little dance of death. Fauns allowed, fawning
verboten. House lights down, and bugger Rimsky."

Waterworks

Imagine, twenty years in America
and I still speak of the soul. I refused
the soldier's mistake: selling my fiddle
to the devil disguised as an old woman.

L.A. was not Paris. By 1962 I'd returned
to Russia triumphant, though meeting
Khrushchev was anything but stellar.
Firebird, Petrushka, Rite of Spring.

When a different rhythm obsessed me,
The Soldier's Tale provided the scope
I required: folksong, jazz, the thrust
of narrative. America was good,

but Venice—ah, Venice. If I speak
of water it's not to claim my soul
is deep, myself well travelled.
Euphrates does not figure here, nor

the Nile with its dhows, grains
of sand finer than cocaine, a youth
pausing to watch the lateen sail
rise amidships, molecules

dusted with desire. Deserts
prevail without music. Pyramids
are what they are and do not require
my talent. What's therapeutic

is the slosh of liquids in the body,
waves lapping the solitary gondola, snug
against a piling. Canals, waterways,
blood, urine, sweat.

Handel saw them as synonymous,
in cahoots. Statues pissing
under Etruscan balconies, human
forms sent into spasm

by vibrating catgut, counterpoint,
harmonics, a poetics of fluidity.
In *L'histoire du soldat*, I played drums
myself, leaving soul-chords

to the soldier and his fiddle. Venice
will do, its quaint mercurial
vespers, sea level high and rising,
and the body mostly water, *da*.

On Being Dead in Venice

Ezra, Ezra, this is no quick pilgrimage
to arrange a few cut roses on your grave
or indulge a little melancholy. So much
to say, so much unfinished business.

In Tintoretto's version of *The Last Supper*,
housed in the sepulchral silence
of the Chiesa di San Giorgio, Christ
and his disciples are stylized, as if

already myth, and claimed by a host
of hovering angels. But the eye, the ravenous
eye, is drawn towards the real, the quotidian,
where a Manx cat stands on its hind legs

to peer into the wicker basket and a serving-
maid, her shoulders naked, reaches into
the container as she offers a plate of olives
to the waiter. She commands more attention

than the saviour, an old man's tribute
to the senses, no doubt, and to simple tasks
of service that otherwise go unnoticed
as dynasties and reputations are made

and unmade. You'd have noticed such things
in your final days, never far from Olga,
beside you now as she was in life. How ironic,
Massimo said as we boarded the commuter train,

you did not know, living in Rapallo, modern
banking was invented not in London or New York
but in Genoa, a few miles away. Would this
have changed your views on Italy or money

lending? Your *Cantos* notwithstanding,
il miglior fabbro did not know everything, caged
in Pisa, tried, then committed to St. Elizabeth
Hospital. Thirteen years, a debt repaid

with interest. Little to distinguish you
in this company: Ingeborg Menkin,
Betty McAndrew, and Sir Ashby Clarke,
ambassador to India and founder

of the Venice in Peril Fund. Venice is
still in peril: sewage, chemicals, tourists,
pollution. As I sit on Sir Ashby's marble slab
with its lion's-claw feet, a pale green gecko

darts from the groundcover to your head-
stone obscuring the Z in Ezra. He's playing
the critic, ushering in The Pound Era.
In low-lying shrubs an acolyte has hung

a plasticized sheet that reads: "Master,
I'm so bored with the USA." You knew,
it seems, even in Hailey, Idaho, that beauty
heals, how in an art so marginal

margins fall away, that taking craft to heart
might still redeem it. Learn from the green
world, you declared at the end: bushes, geckoes,
ground-cover, a Manx cat, décolletage,

preferring song to heroic deeds in Hungary
or Iraq. When they collected you, dishevelled,
in the back garden, a pile of weeds beside you
on the path, the soldiers were surprised,

expecting a tussle, not this ageing scribbler
with his books and bewilderment. Poet, traitor,
and collaborator, found to be of unsound
mind. Your fragments don't cohere,

but make a kind of sense. Vaporetto #42
will drop me on the floating dock in Venice,
but not before I've said goodbye, placed
a stolen plastic flower in the outstretched hand

of the diminutive concrete Christ and piped
the sailor John William Thorington, late
of the *S.S. Tregarthen*, into the Venetian afterlife.
His shipmates erected a granite marker

as his consolation for missing Cathay,
canziones and Lao Tze. He ships out with you,
Ezra, on the waterways of history, art, the storm-
bound straits of high culture, while I return

to Sotoportego di Giovanni in the ghetto
and climb the 95 steps to Giuseppe and Barbara,
radiant with the knowledge she is pregnant,
and a supper I believe is not the last.

Inshallah

And later in that place
they said that when rain fell
horns grew out of the ground.
—Maxamed Xaashi Dhamac 'Gaariye'

Somalia

Not cleanliness freaks, just regular guys
used to having a shower daily. Sand
we knew, for sure, but not old-fashioned
combat, trench mud to the crotch, sharing

the glory with corpses, vermin, lice.
We prided ourselves on not smelling
like the locals. On patrol with my buddy
on the outskirts of Beledweyne we saw

a small boy being doused with ox blood
from a long-handled enamel pot, liquid
cascading down his face and arms, sluicing
his naked back. Mother, in multicoloured

blanket and beads, bent over him as the cure
was administered. In the picture I took
you'll see M. standing in the background,
weapon at rest, his head outside the frame

so you don't see the disgust contorting
his face. The kid must have felt the same,
sceptical, revolted, grossly unclean
as warm blood pooled and clotted in his ears.

Operation Deliverance

This means nothing to the old man
carrying a kettle on his back, handle
looped over a long stick. He's seen it all
before: English, Italians, Germans,
Ethiopians, all wanting something,

beef for Aden, a foothold, a secure port,
disputed land. And now us. We blow
into town, plant our bland maple leaf
in the sand, string barbed wire, flaunt
our weapons, tattoos and girlie

magazines. We're here to deliver them
from themselves, confiscate antique
weapons, exchange clan loyalties
for visions of peace, prosperity, a.k.a.
foreign investment, bases, Coca-Cola

and Christ. The old man, adze draped
over his forearm, does not look at us
as he passes. He's thinking of Allah,
of drought, the glazed eyes of children
he can't feed. *Forty-six words for camel?*

Gimme a break, the sergeant says
as he cracks open a can of beer. *Have
they got a word for decency, for morality?
That asshole probably has four wives
and I can't even get laid. Get a job, buddy.*

So much for cultural awareness training
at home base in Petawawa. Be tough,
they advised us, send a clear signal
to the "crazies." I copied down the essential
notes on crooks, incursions, condoms,

saboteurs. Books were available
even then that would have taught us
something about history, clan values,
how poets might have served us better
here than soldiers. But zip, *rien*.

Monkey Business

What did we know of mythology
out there in the desert? Coyotes,

ravens, trickster figures, how
they take pleasure in havoc,

screw up the best-laid plans,
turn a clear stream blood-red,

and transform a friendly booze-up
into butchery? Scott's monkey

looked innocent enough, leather
collar, eyes closed, soft brown fur,

and one small paw clutching his
dog-tag, half obscuring the tattoo

on Scott's chest. What was going on
behind those smooth, pale lids?

Before the moon had paid its dues
a prowling teen lay bludgeoned

and dead, a string of bloody
spittle drying on his lips,

his last words, *Canada, Canada*,
still hanging in the air.

Letter from Prison

Part One

I'd prefer to dispatch this message on four legs,
a faithful camel worthy of profuse praise.
Noble lineage, generous temperament,
no words spared to describe his vigorous sire,

the cataract of strong sperm, the deep receiving
vulva of a milk-abundant mother. Alas, times
have changed, values too. Now I conjure
taped metaphors for the dilapidated Bedford

van that sets this entreaty on its way, tires
with patches upon patches, paint flaking away
from a constant barrage of sand. Yet its motor's
a heart that doesn't acknowledge distance

or age, delivering power even when drive-shaft
and differential need replacing, or when clutch
and transmission have gone, as our erstwhile allies
the Russians say, *kaput*. Like Muusa, my driver,

who delivers these words and knows the worth
of timing and torque in lorries, if not in poems,
my steadfast Bedford deserves hospitality,
a place to bed down, enjoy a well-earned rest,

a haven with no thought of thieves or vandals,
nourished, inspired by lustful dreams,
pistons thrusting in lubricated cylinders.
Park it, please, with grill and radiator facing

Mecca and the Red Sea. Bedford, I consign you
to good hands. Roar once more at daybreak
like a lion. Or a woman twice wronged.
According to tradition, a herdsman requests

Allah to bless him with obedient wife, swift
horse, ample tent. I was blessed, Alhamdulillah,
with two wives, both disobedient, a concrete
cell for a tent and a cellmate whose only swift

part is his bowel. Would I could pass through
this so-called system of justice as quickly
as the green bile he defecates. I miss the slap
of bread dough and the sting of my first wife's

invective. I know, you warned me. Who listens
to an older brother? I thought you wanted her
yourself. Her insults, delivered in operatic style,
all alliterate. That's devotion, in my books.

Part Two

I don't compose this poem to amuse myself
but to make a small request of you, my brother.
Shidane has been killed by foreign soldiers
in Beledweyne. Yes, the beloved nephew
who hung around your neck, worshipped
your shadow. I'm told he was checking out

the compound, scouting for leftovers, scraps.
Or just curious. What else to do in this climate
of violence? A gentle fellow. If guilty of theft,
would not a single hand suffice? Do they care
about our customs, these intruders? No, they fire
on crowds, crash vehicles into tents, confiscate

heirlooms and, alas, defile our young girls
in Mogadishu. Are you not *ninhadal*, a man
of words? Hear my request. Speak to the colonel,
the one with the French name. He'll heed an elder
like yourself. His country must pay restitution,
dyya, and acknowledge its guilt in the public

eye. Then, perhaps, I'll die in peace, if peace
is not a stranger to this place. Allah willing,
I'll come to you again, repair the damage done
when young, foolish and a Dervish remnant,
I rode against you in the Ogaden, more patriot
than kinsman. Only the hyena triumphs

on the field of battle, the perfect democrat,
eating enemies as equals. Let's find a way
to do things differently, disarm a grievance
with a gift, end *godob*, reciprocal vendettas
that perpetuate the spin, the cycle of pain.
Forgive the travesty of sending to you

a taped message. My faithful driver, Muusa,
lacks skill as a reciter. He remembers to pray
daily and to check the Bedford's oil and gas,
but all words, dull or beautiful, escape him,
drown in his ears. What you'll hear at least
approximates my voice. I trust its grating rasp

elicits a smile and recalls a lost childhood
when we rode camels, scoffed at the behaviour
of elders. I can still see your hair blown back
as you bend into the wind. I've advised Muusa
to store this tape away from batteries, electric
wires. Let hatred only be erased, Inshallah.

Afterwords

The Resumption of Play takes its name from a line uttered by the speaker in the title poem, at a residential school on the B.C. coast, where Indigenous children waited in the schoolyard for the priest to call a number from his window on the fourth floor. When the unlucky owner of that number disappeared, play could resume. However, the title has two other connotations for me, one more important than the other. First, the title also alludes, at least in my mind, to the gradual release of Indigenous survivors from the tragic and tyrannical legacy of the residential schools, where their lives ceased to have meaning and where their self-respect either died or went underground. Now the public can begin to understand and acknowledge what this legacy has contributed to the dysfunction and pain of First Nations, Métis and Inuit families and communities, a new sense of freedom and dignity beginning for all of us.

I use the word 'play' quite deliberately, as humour has been a survival mechanism for Indigenous peoples in Canada. Learning how to navigate the shoals of all that deadly ritual, abuse and withholding required talent. Some kids learned to steal the food they needed; others imitated the gestures and speech of their captors while developing a sign language to communicate with each other when their own tongue was forbidden. They had hiding places and nicknames for their keepers and abusers. Even now, as racism continues in Canada, only humour and traditional discipline keep our Indigenous brothers and sisters and other peoples of colour, from outward expressions of violence. For those who have not learned these survival games, the violence is often turned against themselves, their family or community.

Finally, this book represents, for me, a welcome shift from a decade or more of non-fiction writing, where content can so often override or overshadow form, back to the more open and playful fields of poetry. I've resumed here the use of persona, which has long allowed me to escape (or explore more deeply) a few of the inhibitions and limitations imposed by my own ego and to investigate a broader range of emotions and concerns than was otherwise possible. Large non-fiction projects are usually funded by commercial presses hoping for a return on their investment. While this is not surprising, it does impose certain limitations on the writer, eliminating many of those lateral shifts—jazz riffs—that are so engaging and illuminating in poetry. Back home in the poetic hinterlands, an aside is not necessarily an affront.

So I have felt free enough again to bring together poems about the loss of my mother, who died when she was thirty-five and I was seven. A long overdue conversation took place between us, a few pieces of which have made their way into this book. My tribute to Virginia Woolf, who achieved so much in spite of her mental illness, holds hands here with a small lyric about one of my favourite Canadian poets, Bronwen Wallace, giving so much of herself to needy friends even as cancer eroded the rest. The lives and voices of women fascinate me, also their struggle to contend with and educate men; two of those voices demanded to be heard here.

The Somalia Affair, which prompted my immersion in African politics, but which became only a minor thread in *Drink the Bitter Root*, left a few things unsaid, in particular a two-part letter from prison to a brother on the outside that just might reflect some of the feelings of the father of Shidane Abukar Arone, the young Somali teenager tortured and murdered by members of the Canadian Airborne Regiment stationed in Beledweyne. I hope the values of Somali society—namely, dignity and honour—are reflected in these letters, along with a few hints of their highly rhetorical poetic style.

Freedom and play don't often come to mind when you think of death, unless, of course, your life has been a disaster and you view the afterlife as a release. For the believers amongst us, with whom I don't count myself, heaven would be the obvious spot for a resumption of play. What I'm thinking of here, however, is the message of art itself which, less burdened by biographical clatter and the tyranny of ideas, can have a life of its own. This is what fascinated me about the case of Ezra Pound, a brilliant poet whose observations about Jews and money lending eroded his authority and damaged his reputation as a poet. That he shares a cemetery in Venice with three famous Russian artists—Joseph Brodsky, Igor Stravinsky and Sergei Diaghilev—provided fertile ground for some thoughts on the playground where art and ideology duke it out. Or do their complicated dance.

Acknowledgements

I would like to thank the juries and editors who selected some of these poems for publication, prizes and shortlists. "Vodorosli" appeared in *The Bow-Wow Shop, A Poetry Emporium*; "At Swim Three Words" and "Late Breaking News" were shortlisted for the Montreal Poetry Prize and appeared in their anthologies; "Intertidal" was shortlisted for the Troubadour International Poetry Competition in London; "Inshallah" was shortlisted in the Arvon International Poetry Competition. And the title poem, "The Resumption of Play," shared first prize in *The Malahat Review* Long Poem competition, appearing in the June 2015 issue of the magazine.

I would also like to thank my wife Ann Eriksson and the many friends who read these poems and offered helpful comments: Di Brandt, Ron Smith, Ross Leckie, Andrew Mitchell, Jim Anderson, Paul DePasquale, Chris Knight, and especially my publisher and eagle-eyed editor Allan Briesmaster.

About the Author

Gary Geddes was born in Vancouver and worked on the coast as a fisherman, water-taxi driver and warehouseman before taking up teaching and writing. He has written and edited more than 45 books of poetry, fiction, drama, non-fiction, criticism, translation and anthologies and has been the recipient of a dozen national and international literary awards, including the Commonwealth Poetry Prize (Americas Region), National Magazine Gold Award, Writers Choice Award, the Lt.-Governor's Award for Literary Excellence and the Gabriela Mistral Prize, awarded simultaneously to Octavio Paz, Václav Havel, Ernesto Cardenal, Rafael Alberti and Mario Benedetti. His most recent works are the non-fiction book, *Drink the Bitter Root: A writer's search for justice and redemption in Africa* and three poetry books: *Falsework*, *Swimming Ginger* and a book of selected poems called *What Does A House Want?*

Geddes taught at Concordia University in Montreal and has since served as Distinguished Professor of Canadian Culture at Western Washington University in Bellingham and visiting writer at the University of Missouri-St. Louis and many institutions in Canada. He is the author of a book of essays, *Out of the Ordinary: Politics, Poetry & Narrative*; and his poetry is the subject of a series of critical articles, *Gary Geddes: Essays on His Works*, edited by Robert G. May. He lives on Thetis Island and is married to biologist and novelist Ann Eriksson.

Other Recent Quattro Poetry Books